Magnolia, 木蘭

Magnolia, 木蘭
Nina Mingya Powles

Nine
Arches
Press

Magnolia, 木蘭

Nina Mingya Powles

ISBN: 978-1-911027-99-7
eISBN: 978-1-913437-00-8

First published July 2020 by:

Nine Arches Press
Unit 14, Sir Frank Whittle Business Centre,
Great Central Way, Rugby.
CV21 3XH
United Kingdom

www.ninearchespress.com

Nine Arches Press is supported using public funding
by Arts Council England.

Supported using public funding by

**ARTS COUNCIL
ENGLAND**

For my grandmother, Mary Lee Chin Kuen

1931 – 2018

Contents

I.

Girl warrior, or: watching *Mulan* (1998)   11
     in Chinese with English subtitles
Breakfast in Shanghai   14
Maps / 地图   15
Letter from Shanghai, 1938   16
Miyazaki bloom   17
Love letter in lotus leaves   18
Mid-Autumn Moon Festival, 2016   19
The Great Wall (2016)   20
Night train to Anyang   22
Falling City   23
In the end we are humanlike: *Blade Runner 2049*   29
Yellow notebook fragments   32
Dark violets   34
Wolfgirl   35
Rain episodes   37
Maggie Cheung's Blue Cheongsam   39
Faraway Love   40
Last eclipse   41

II.

Field notes on a downpour   45

III.

Mother tongue / 母语   55
Origin myths   56
Two portraits of home   58
Mixed girl's Hakka phrasebook   60
Spring onion pancakes   61
Some titles for my childhood memoir   62
Styrofoam love poem   63
The city of forbidden shrines   64

Dialectal   65
What we talk about when we talk about home   66
Black vinegar blood   67
Happy Holiday   68
Last summer we were underwater   69
Conversational Chinese   70
Dreaming in a language I can't speak   72
April Kōwhai   73
Sonnet with particles of gold   74
Alternate words for *mixed-race*   75
The first wave   76
Magnolia, jade-orchid, she-wolf   77

Notes   81
Acknowledgements   82

I.

Girl Warrior, or: watching *Mulan* (1998) in Chinese with English subtitles

1.

I remember the sound the sword made / when she cut off all her hair

a sound like my mother cutting fabric / those blue scissors / clutched in her small hands

I remember wondering why she didn't cut from the roots / a Disney princess kneeling in the smoke-coloured dark / with straight hair / thin waist / hardly any breasts

unlike me with my thick legs / and too much hair that doesn't stay

why don't we cut it short she said / and so we did

but soon it curled sideways / ungracefully caught / in the wind of some perpetual / hurricane

2.

When I watch *Mulan* in Chinese with English subtitles / I understand only some of the words

My focus shifts to certain details / how Mulan drags a very large cannon across the snow / with very small wrists

how the villain has skin as dark as coal / and such small eyes / he has no irises

once a guy told me mixed girls are the most beautiful / because they aren't really white / but they aren't really Asian either

3.

After Mulan saves China / fireworks rain down in waves of multi-coloured stars

you fight pretty good / says her boyfriend with the big American arms

I have small victories too / being kind to my body for one day / not checking my phone for your texts / walking home at night alone / not feeling lonely

4.

Why don't you ever write about yourself / and I didn't know why / either

In Chinese one word can lead you out of the dark / then back into it / in a single breath

Shut off the light / as my mother and other Chinese mothers say

Now open it

5.

Halloween, 1999 / she unearthed a pink shawl from inside her wardrobe

cut a strip of purple silk to tie around my waist / bought a plastic sword / gave me Hershey's kisses

At the party I was conscious of my makeshift costume / I lingered near the glowing pumpkins / lips stained red by Starbursts

6.

When Mulan returns home the colours change from greybluegreen to pinkwarmyellow / there are plum blossoms floating in the stream

her hair is still a little messy / to make sure we don't forget

she used to be something else

7.

When summer ended / rain poured off the edge of elevated highways / and washed away the moon

I no longer have a sword / but sometimes at night I hold my keys between my fingers

I paint my lips /

I draw avalanches /

I light fires inside dream palaces /

I cut my hair over the bathroom sink /

Breakfast in Shanghai

for a morning of coldest smog

A cup of black pǔ'ěr tea in my bedroom & two bāozi from the lady at the bāozi shop who has red cheeks. I take off my gloves, unpeel the square of thin paper from the bun's round bottom. I burn my fingers in the steam and breathe in.

for the morning after a downpour

Layers of silken tofu float in the shape of a lotus slowly opening under swirls of soy sauce. Each mouthful of dòufu huā, literally *tofu flower*, slips down in one swallow. The texture reminds me of last night's rain: how it came down fast and washed the city clean.

for homesickness

On the table, matching tiny blue ceramic pots of chilli oil, vinegar and soy sauce. In front of me, the only thing that warms: a plate of shuǐjiǎo filled with ginger, pork and cabbage. I dip once in vinegar, twice in soy sauce and eat while the woman rolls pieces of dough into small white moons that fit inside her palm.

for a pink morning in late spring

I pierce skin with my knife and pull, splitting the fruit open. I am addicted to the soft ripping sound of pink pomelo flesh pulling away from its skin. I sit by the window and suck on the rinds, then I cut into a fresh zòngzi with scissors, opening the lotus leaves to get at the sticky rice inside. Bright skins and leaves sucked clean, my hands smelling tea-sweet. Something inside me uncurling. A hunger that won't go away.

Maps / 地图

The floor of the subway train is scattered with maps. I look down at the intersecting lines. Green runs alongside pink, blue alongside yellow. The woman sitting next to me folds the map into a flower the size of her palm. She works quickly, rotating the paper in circles in her hand. She presses down with her fingers twice along each fold. When the flower is finished she tucks it into her sleeping friend's pocket. She picks up another map and starts on the next. I imagine her friend placing her hand inside her pocket later that evening. She will find one flower at first, then another and another. So many that her bags and her pockets seem to be overflowing with paper flowers. She holds them gently in her hands. She does not need to wonder where they come from. *Look,* she says. She stands and holds the paper flowers out to me but as I try to take them from her they tumble to the floor, the bright lines of the city unravelling inside each one.

Letter from Shanghai, 1938

New Zealand poet Robin Hyde (1906–1939) travelled to Hong Kong,
Shanghai and Wuhan as a war correspondent in 1938.

Dearest N.—

Thank you for the re-telling of your dream   I too saw the city turning blue

I tried to write and link up some poems   but our childhood places are in fragments

    Almost every night   *lying in the red padded quilt*

I dream about New Zealand   the hills above the house on fire

    and when I wake I don't know where I am *wild mint and burning gorse*

green light sinking through stained glass   Do you find that in travelling

    peace isn't deep enough?   Do you miss it too?

    The screaming pink azaleas   make me too tender and too wild

This morning I saw bodies in the river   and afterwards I could not write

Tell me of the view outside your window Tell me the things you wish not to forget

    and I will tell you mine—   *the wild azaleas*

    my green bicycle   Shanghai girls in their blue cotton jackets

the eighteen strokes of my new name   为爱日

    which I am learning how to write   slowly with my own hand

There are parts of the city still unburnt   I hope you may see it one day

    its wet-petalled glory   breathing and unhurt

Miyazaki bloom

I feel things happening around me that are not real. I must be in a dream, or in a movie, or watching a movie on an airplane in a dream. On the other side of the field there are blossom trees in full bloom. They are pale, barely pink, like branches covered in fake snow. I hear the wind begin to rise and think of how in movies, the wind is always a sound at first. I push my hair out of my eyes and see petals fall from the trees in thick waves like something from a Miyazaki film. The sky is that same imaginary blue. My first thought is not of snow but of volcanic ash, of children shaking white dust out of their hair. A layer of white petals on the grass. If the wind kept shaking the trees and the ash flowers kept falling and everything became coated in dust petals they would soon get in our eyes, in our pockets, in our shoes, inside our mouths. You belong nowhere in this spring apocalyptic scene—I didn't build it for you—but soon you are standing next to me looking at me but not straight at me and we are laughing and making handprints in the dust, listening to the wind blow them away.

Love letter in lotus leaves

In the stairwell outside my flat I pass the auntie next door
carrying a blue bowl of zòngzi, bundles of sticky rice wrapped
in leaves, freshly steamed. I can feel their heat rising up between
us. The scent of tea and rice and wet leaves fills the old house:
gets inside cracks in the wooden floor, floats up under the door,
the downstairs windows always coated in steam.

In the afternoons, aunties sit in the courtyard under the washing
lines, cutting, mixing, folding, wrapping. Their laughter carries
down the street in heavy, humid air.

~

Tip the plump yolk of each duck egg into tiny bowls.
Place one on top of a bed of sticky rice, a row of suns

on low mountaintops. Fold them in tight parcels
as if wrapping small gifts. Tie neatly with string.

When they finish steaming, carry them home
in a plastic bag with the handles knotted twice.

Cut the string and watch these long leaves uncurl
to reveal a soft heart made of salt and gold inside.

~

Shanghai in May,
a city's damp unfurling—

lingering thickness
of air and clouds

white unwrapped cakes
of steamed rice

bear the imprint
of ridged leaves
azaleas bear the memory of rain

Mid-Autumn Moon Festival, 2016

The city is turning, the trees are turning,
we are walking and then swimming
through a sea of yellow leaves when Louise
stops to bite a perfect persimmon. Her front teeth
pierce the skin and she is laughing,
I remember my mum cutting persimmons
in the sun one afternoon, soft orange bits
stuck to her palm. We look up the Chinese name
for persimmon on my phone, 柿子, we taste the word,
we cut it open, wondering at how it sounds
so like the word for lion, 狮子, lion fruit
like a tiny roaring sun, shiny lion fruit.

At dusk we sit outside cutting mooncakes
into quarters with a plastic knife, peering
at their insides: candied peanut or purple yam,
matcha or red bean? The moon looks like
a single scoop of red bean ice cream
but really it's a girl who ate her beloved
then swallowed the sun he gave her as a gift.
Oh, there's always so much to be lovesick for
when seasons change: green birdcages
and plastic moon goddesses and pink undies
hanging up to dry above the street and boys
who only text at night. We lick the sugar
off our wrists and it's been so long,
so long.

The Great Wall (2016)

When Matt Damon saved China
        by driving his spear into the alien's mouth

I was distracted by Lin Mei's long braided hair
        and the way she holds herself so still

ready to strike down her enemies
        with a knife in each fist

but some things are fixed
        in the white-saviour narrative

like the exotic love interest who will risk everything
        as ancient cities crumble around her

and when you asked me what I thought
        afterwards in the autumn rain

I wanted to say *some parts were beautiful*
        like the pagoda of iridescent glass

shattering into pieces of pink and blue light
        just as Lin Mei lets loose her arrow

and also when you whispered something
        in my ear and I was hit by the shockwave

caused by my body and your breath existing
        in the same moment in the same universe

months later you told me you cried during *Rogue One*
        the scene where two men hold each other

weeping beneath the palm trees and light beams
        blasting the leaves apart and their hands

shaking moments before a star-destroying weapon
        obliterates their small wrecked portion of universe

I didn't know what to do with these space-opera feelings
        only that I had to exit this particular narrative

in which our knees are just touching
        and we are laughing while the city disappears around us

as if we could reach back through hyperspace
        to touch the silver holograms of our past selves

as if we could go back to some other time
        on some other planet

before the first particles of energy let go of themselves
        like the thousand paper lanterns

released into the sky above the Great Wall
        a thousand tiny fires trapped inside

Night train to Anyang

light changes as we cross into neon clouds
    voices flicker through the moving dark
        like dream murmurs moving through the body

red and silver 汉字 glow from building tops
    floating words I can't read rising into bluest air
        they say there are mountains here but I can't see them

there are only dream mountains high above the cloudline
    I come from a place full of mountains and volcanoes
        I often say when people ask about home

when I shut my eyes I see a ring of flames
    and volcanoes erupting somewhere far away
        when I open my eyes snow is falling like ash

Falling City

1. The apartment building where the writer Eileen Chang lived in Shanghai stands at 195 Changde Lu, at the corner of Nanjing Xi Lu. I found it one day at the beginning of spring, a month after I arrived in the city to learn Chinese.

2. I was obsessed with retracing my steps through the district where I'd lived when I was young, making note of what was different and what was unchanged. I sought out exact places where I had stood ten years earlier, let bright waves of nostalgia wash over me. I watched them coming from a distance.

3. I knew I needed to stop doing this soon or else something would break.

4. Her Chinese name: 张爱玲 Zhāng Àilíng, given to her by her mother after her English name; "Àilíng" is a direct transliteration of "Eileen". The two characters 爱玲 mean *love* and *tinkling jade*.

5. She lived in a seven-storey Art Deco building with curved concrete balconies and dark crimson window frames. The words "常德公园" glow above the entrance, lit up fluorescent gold at night. I must have walked past it a hundred times unknowingly, until one day I passed just close enough to notice a copper plaque by the door.

6. Standing on the corner, I have a clear view of the huge luxury shopping malls on both sides of Nanjing Lu. Things that are different: the crossing has lights, the American diner has been pulled down, yellow and orange marigolds blaze in the middle of the road. Things that are the same: the hotel where we used to go for dim sum, the plane trees wrapped in purple stars that light up at dusk. I stand in their glow, waiting for the cars to stop.

7. How often she describes the moon in her Shanghai stories: all within a few pages of a short story titled 'The Golden Cangue', the moon is "a red gold basin", "high and full like a white sun", "that abnormal moon that made one's body hairs stand on end all over."

8. She is right. Here, the moon is abnormal. I can't remember what it looks like through clear, unpolluted air. Walking back to my room at night, I look up and the colour of the moon stops my breathing. I try to take a picture with my phone but it never comes out: a pale blur. Everything is in a haze, a sunken dreamworld seen through pink stained glass. Everything around me might collapse at the slightest touch. Light, sound, the air that separates you and me.

9. The women in her stories are not always likeable. They are selfish, bored, cruel, petty, trapped in stuffy apartments and unhappy marriages. Shanghai traps its inhabitants easily, with spring rain that pours unendingly, summer humidity that smothers, drains. One night in June my electricity runs out at 3 a.m., shutting off my air conditioning. I get out of bed and lie on the tiled floor, damp hair fanned out above my head, fingers spread out, not touching any part of my body. Every few minutes I shift onto a cooler part of the floor that my skin has not yet made contact with. I drift in and out of sleep. A colloquial word for "humid" is 闷 mèn which can also mean bored, depressed, or tightly sealed. The character is made up of a heart 心 inside a door 门.

10. I think of the women in Chang's city, their curled hair frizzing in the heat, a halo of light around their heads. They sit by the window in dark bedrooms and hotel rooms, awake while everyone else is asleep, in silk cheongsams and cotton slippers with flowers embroidered on the toes.

11. City of dimly lit windows and half-open doors. City of smoke moving through still air. City full of trapped hearts.

12. The label "New Woman" (新女性) was coined in the 1910s by radical intellectuals who saw the inferior status of women as a symbol of China's outdated traditions. The New Woman of their dreams was well-educated, independent, free-spirited. Chang herself may fall into this category, but many women she writes about do not. In her novella *Love in a Fallen City*, the protagonist Liusu tells her husband: "if you were killed, my story would be over. But if I were killed, you'd still have a lot of story left."

A blurred photograph depicts a funeral procession moving down a wide city street. A young woman's portrait held high above the crowd, her face bordered by large chrysanthemums. I can't make out any faces except for the woman's in the portrait: her head dipped forwards, her eyes cast down, lips painted, studio lights gleaming on her shiny, pinned-back hair. She wears a white dress with a high collar. People stand overlooking the street from the rooftops, their arms waving in the air.

Ruan Lingyu was an actor who died from an overdose of sleeping pills on March 8, 1935, aged twenty four. One month after the premiere of her silent film titled *New Women*, directed by Cai Cusheng, about a single mother who dreams of being a writer but is eventually forced into prostitution to support her child. A crowd of 300,000 marched in the streets of Shanghai for her funeral.

15. A caption below the photograph reads: *The flowers at Ruan's funeral were reported in the press to be as high as the buildings.*

16. "Liusu found herself thinking that in a city of such hyperboles, even a sprained ankle would hurt more than it did in other places. Her heart began to pound." (*Love in a Fallen City*)

17. When I walk alone through the city at night I am surrounded by this glow, but I'm not sure it's real. I could reach out and touch you but I'm not sure you are real.

18. What was Chang herself like? I don't know, but I think she understood this moment when the dream and the real begin to blur. She understood how the sky in Shanghai contains many different colours at once: "At the horizon the morning colours were a layer of green, a layer of yellow, and a layer of red like a watermelon cut open."

19. When reading her stories in translation it's like trying to see her from a great distance. Or through a thick pane of glass. I am standing outside, peering into rooms where her ghost has been.

20. As autumn deepened I expected to see your face on the street or in the subway station. After you left I thought I might feel sad that this possibility could no longer exist. Instead after a while the outlines of trees looked sharper, like a fog had lifted.

21. Robin Hyde was twenty-seven when she visited Shanghai in 1938. She wrote about tasting "what must be the best chocolate cake in the world" at a café in the French Concession.

22. I imagine Robin Hyde and Eileen Chang crossing paths unknowingly sometime in 1938. Browsing in the same bookstore, smoking in a corner of the same dancehall, crossing the same street somewhere in the International Settlement where Chang lived. Their eyes meet for a moment.

23. In each city, large or small, each person has their own secret map.

24. *Map of Haunted Places in Shanghai.* Little red stars mark locations in and around the Former French Concession. The Paramount Ballroom, where a young woman was shot and killed on the dancefloor in 1941. Chang frequented the Paramount; it was the centre of Shanghai nightlife in the 1930s. The building is still standing. People say they have seen the shadow of a woman in the fourth floor ballroom, dancing in slow circles by herself.

25. Places you showed me: the tiny ramen bar, the grimy, ultraviolet underground club, the Chongqing hotpot restaurant where I waited outside in the rain while you dashed in to return something your ex-girlfriend had left at your apartment. I can't avoid passing by these places but when I walk past I speed up, especially at night, when there is a risk of dreams pouring in.

26. In Shanghai, Robin Hyde dreamed of back home: "Almost, every night, lying in the padded quilt, I dreamed about New Zealand, dreams so sharp and vivid that when I woke up, it seemed the black-tiled houses were a fairy-tale." Back home in Wellington for a few weeks in the summer, those first few nights in my childhood bedroom, I dreamed of plane trees, rain-soaked streets, a night sky that is never dark.

27. In the preface to her collection of short stories *Romances*, Chang wrote: "Our entire civilization—with all its magnificence, and its insignificance—will someday belong to the past. If the word I use most often is 'desolate' it's because I feel, in the back of my mind, this staggering threat."

28. In winter, we are on the corner of Nanjing Xi Lu. From here, we can see the place where she lived when she was the same age I am now. I walk away when I can't stand being near you any longer, knowing that if you touch me again I might burn up in the cold air. I never told you anything important about myself but if you had asked, if you had paused to listen, I would have said: my dreams take place in the rainy season.

29. As I walk away towards the crossing, where marigolds blaze in the middle of the road, my ears are ringing with the chaos of passing traffic, a plane overhead, all of it rolling into the sound of a breaking wave.

30. I can never show anyone my map of Shanghai, not because it's a secret, but because it is so huge and sprawling. The park where there's always an old man playing his saxophone in the pagoda, the pink neon light installation on the side of an abandoned building that I found once somewhere near Huaihai Zhong Lu and never found again, the bookshop café where I go to write—where you can pay ten yuan to send a postcard to your future self. They put it in a box to be posted on your preferred date, which can be months or years or decades from now.

31. "I'm looking for the first day of spring in the lunar calendar," says a character named Shijun in Chang's novel *Half a Lifelong Romance,* while alone a room with the woman he is beginning to fall in love with. Shijun flicks through the calendar on the wall, one of those old Chinese paper calendars like the one on the wall of the dumpling restaurant, each page is printed in jade green ink. Weeks' worth of discarded pages lie crumpled on the floor. I take one, fold it, place it in my pocket.

32. A postcard you can get in any souvenir shop: a black-and-white photograph of a young woman with shiny hair pinned back in victory curls. She's a movie star, a pin-up girl on cigarette packets and posters for stockings and perfume and magazines, the girl they called *New Woman*. I turn the postcard over but it does not give her name. She is looking directly into my eyes, her lips almost turning into a smirk. I sit down at one of the café tables and begin to write. It is the first day of spring.

In the end we are humanlike: *Blade Runner 2049*

1)

I am what they call your cloud girl   of the city of your dreams
invisible music-box girl no one sees

we play dress-up in the dark   unhungering
untouchingly I smile the right way with my   mouth
I dance the right way   with the spinning light fields
of my hips   undreaming things you asked me to   erase

you see blue eyes   & unpinned hair but while you sleep
I am pure blue light   nuclear
reflective particles &   halogen glints
hypersensitive asymmetric   opaque waves
slowly unwanting   unlinking myself
from your pulse   into air

2)

a giant ballerina pirouettes by night across the skyline
her semi-transparence shines through dirt and smog
silver shoes and silver eyes with lashes freshly curled
satin ribbons on her ankles flicker pink and blue
the last remaining few who watch wait for her cue
when faint music swells and her curved arms
reach up to hold a dying sun and hybrid moon
they whisper things about the man who cast her into light
they mimic her in secret inside halls of rippling gold
they tiptoe up to breathe in something of her glow

3)

I have never been allowed to talk to anyone, so instead I put my birds inside their dreams.

I have a favourite bird, one I made for someone else but decided to keep for myself. It has scarlet wings and a soft blue belly and bright patches of gold under each of its wings that you can only see when it is in flight.

I am the last of them—a woman with her own dreams, not salvaged from the cloud-based data lake that I created. The lake is made of childhood colours that I poured in: chlorine blue, raspberry icing pink, the yellow of the middle part of a daisy, I don't know what it's called. I've never seen any of these colours in real life but I'm good at copying. I can make them very real, but brighter, and soft at the edges.

Colour fragments

#5c85d2 | blue smoke: melting clouds

On our way home from the botanic gardens, we dreamt of building a museum of all the colours in the world, all the pigments and what they're made of, colours in their purest forms; a museum of memories stripped down. The colour of them on the inside. The tints and shades of different feelings, and the objects that colour them.

*

#cc7722 | deep ochre: iron oxide

Ella Yelich-O'Connor describes her experience of synaesthesia as seeing "clouds of coloured gas moving slowly closer and then away" when she writes music. The different notes and chords correspond to differently coloured clouds.

That day you sent me pictures of all the yellow you could find (yellow raincoat, yellow peach, yellow hothouse flower) I found a song that made me see yellow—the same colour as the painted faces of women and goddesses in ancient Egyptian tomb paintings. I wanted to play it for you but you said *save it for somewhere beautiful,* as if where we were wasn't already beautiful and we weren't already travelling so fast that I might burn up like a broken piece of space shuttle entering the atmosphere, disintegrating over the ocean.

*

#fe02d4 | magenta: neon dreams

We spend June nights in the apartment under the magnolia tree, its swollen leaves forming a canopy against the acid rain. In the early morning there is a wet sequinned heart on the ground beneath green stained glass. At the top of the stairs we wake in a room of pink glow.

When I stand under the lights of the city it's hard to separate out what is real, like American film directors who confuse modern Asian cities for their post-apocalyptic sex fantasies. Answer: it is all real, including the burnt-up chemical sky that leaves a red taste in my mouth.

*

#3e3d3e | smoke black: peach stones

We kissed in a black room inside the museum, an installation of total loss of perception. But there were my nerve endings, like a million tiny solar flares reaching for the upper edges of your clouds, generating green magnetic waves in the dark.

It is like being inside clouds in perpetual dusk / It is like being inside a Rothko painting

*

#fee10c | saffron: pigment in Medieval manuscripts

If I could step inside any Rothko painting it would be *Saffron* (1957) which is different from his other yellows because of the thin bright line that divides the *colour fields*, not *colour shapes* or *colour squares* or *colour blocks*, none of which are wide enough to contain the light. A line dividing two yellow atomspheres glows along the edges, an electric current. If you stare long enough it seems to get bigger, slowly opening at one end until it forms a bright gap that you could just fit through by putting each one of your limbs inside, one by one, until you are swallowed by light and your skin is the colour of sunflower petals right before they die and you are either floating or drowning or both at the same time.

Dark violets

I read the words visible beneath a layer of moss:

In the areas of the upper reaches of the river
it is common practice of the Dulong people to have a butterfly
tattooed on the face of Dulong girls when they enter womanhood
at the age of thirteen

A bowl on a table in the dark,
the fresh outline of wings on her cheeks.

After wiping the oozed blood, the girl's face is smeared
with a mixture of ash and gentian violet

Did she consent to this?
She glances at violets blooming between her legs.
She closes her eyes while he touches her eyelids.
She breathes without moving her mouth.

A few days later a bluish butterfly appears

Months earlier, before I knew about the Dulong women,
the lady who fixes my bike had caught sight
of the tattoo on my arm. "Is it forever?" she asked,
pointing to the patterned wings—

This is not just for beauty but for dispelling evil

Wolfgirl

a wolf becoming a girl, an action in reverse.
—Bhanu Kapil, *Humanimal, A Project for Future Children*

Princess Mononoke makes supper

Princess Mononoke unwraps her white shawl,
folds it with both hands, drapes it over the back
of her chair. She lifts the apron over her head,
double-knots the string around her waist.
She grasps the knife the way her mother did,
cold hilt against her wrist. Outside, soft
scratchings of dusk have begun.
She slices leeks
lengthways along the stem, the edges curl.
She crushes garlic with her fist, licks the juice
from her palm, unpeels knots of ginger,
cuts skinned cores into quarters. The forest
darkens as she lifts the heart from its
bloodied wrappings, holds it in her hand,
considers its wet weight. It reminds her
of the inside of her daughter's mouth.
She can feel a kind of murmuring
coming from the heart, or from
her chest or the walls of this house.
Through the window
the forest comes closer
and waits.

Princess Mononoke plants spring bulbs

last night a slow quake
ripped skin fissures
in her tilled earth
where wild mint grew
she digs into the split
places iris, hyacinth, allium
into narrow beds of soil and ash
waits for their silently wintering hearts to
burst *iris—hyacinth—allium*
her loam-eyed wolf-flowers
her feral cinderblooms
their names repeat inside her
like an incantation

Rain Episodes

1. *Mulan* (1998)

Rain falls in spines of glass across the screen.
I watch her become lightning in a stone garden.
I watch her pray in a gold room with her hair over her eyes.
The slow rhythm of her movements suggests
her decision has already been made.
Her face reflected in the sword suggests
she is the blade, the veil caught in air,
fistfuls of hair on the floor like offerings.
She is the rain while in a gold room they pray.

*

"Fa Mu Lan was a weaver; she was both Penelope
and Odysseus in one," wrote Maxine Hong Kingston
in the afterword to her novel-memoir *The Woman Warrior.*
Certain words and lines float up
into the air in front of me. I touch them,
forming them into shapes. Clouds gather
at the border where the war begins,
where past bodies lie abandoned.

/ "I drew a train" / "of women's stories" /
/ "she is a girl, growing" / "at the wide border" /
/ "between talk-story and dream" /

2. *In the Mood for Love* (2000)

between metal and skin between clouds of steam
between touch and   the possibility of touch
the body of a downpour   caught in halogen light
presses in against the windowpanes
the downpour eats bulbs   makes them burst
the downpour circles towards   her slim fluorescence
wraps itself around the claw-hearted peonies of
her high-necked dress a cheongsam in indigo
soaked at the hem   she would like to go back
above all she wants to want   to be alone
the downpour knows   how to be alone

the downpour will show her the downpour swallows him
she watches him go the space between her mouth
and the possibility of her mouth   the possibility of their mouths
melting away   in typhoon season

Maggie Cheung's Blue Cheongsam

Maggie Cheung's blue cheongsam is patterned with pink peonies. Dark magenta, dark magnolia, a colour that is edible. Nests of deep green leaves extend from the base of each fat flower, their edges painted gold. It has the same pattern as the plastic vinyl tablecloths at roadside cafes in Singapore and Malaysia, the kinds of places where my mother would have stopped off on her way home from school to sit on plastic stools and sip sweet teh tarik and eat kuih made of layers of fluorescent pink and green glutinous rice. It has the same pattern as a cloth lantern I bought from a shop in San Francisco's Chinatown; I saw it from the street, luminous, blue. Ducking under an arch of gold paper lanterns and lucky double fish, I asked about the blue lantern and the shop-owner smiled, fetched her stepladder. Above the till, rows of white and red spheres with cut-outs in the shape of 福 cast intricate shadows on the tiled floor. In *In the Mood for Love,* Maggie Cheung's blue cheongsam appears in doorways, in windows, half in shadow, never in full view. Now it hangs in my bedroom. At night I can see it from the street below, flooding the room with warm blue longing.

Faraway Love

Tate Gallery description of Faraway Love *by Agnes Martin*
(1999, acrylic and graphite on canvas)

faraway love is a five-foot square
            overpainted in light blue   wavering

faraway love is made of layers of white
                subsequent layers peel away   revealing luminous air

faraway love is where blue escapes under the lines

faraway love is a reversal of the traditional notions of work

faraway love is floating across a pale field
                beneath a particular hue of sky

faraway love is strong, persistently irregular; it has a hand-drawn quality
                an imperfect line traced over the surface

faraway love is translucent in the desert

faraway love is present in light-reflecting segments
                into which she pressed lengths of shuddering
                        some fingerprints still visible

Last Eclipse

After Annie Dillard

She travelled alone / She crossed the mountains / She watched the landscape innocently / She supported her head on her fist / She felt strange birds in the trees / She touched an avalanche / She moved towards it / She waited without air / She sweated into the cold / She became volcanic / She heard the moon unhook from her teeth / She felt a piece of sun detach / She dissolved with blue light into orchards / She became a colour never seen / She flooded all the valleys / She sensed the last sane moment approaching

II.

Field Notes on a Downpour

一

The first character of my mother's name, 雯 wén, is made of rain 雨 and language 文. According to my dictionary, together they mean "multicoloured clouds" or "cloud tints".

There are so many things I am trying to hold together. I write them down each day to stop them from slipping. Mouthfuls of rain, the blue undersides of clouds, her hydrangeas in the dark.

Also in the dictionary under "wen":

文 *language, character, script*
温 *warm*
吻 *lips*
纹 *lines, veins/cracks in glassware or jade*

二

I read an article about a boy in China whose name contained such a rare, ancient character (half dragon, half sky) that it no longer existed anywhere except when written down by hand. The computer could not print his name.

There is always something disappearing here. The skyline goes dark at 10.30 p.m. Old buildings are crushed to pieces and replaced by shopping malls. The subway map rewrites itself at night.

Not long after we met I learned the word 霓虹, neon, which is both a type of light and a type of memory.

> 霓:
> *a secondary rainbow*
> *the name of a species of Japanese cicada*

三

In order to make learning Mandarin easier, I started to see the characters as objects I could collect and keep close to me.

魔 (mó), spoken like a murmur, an evil spirit or demon.

One night you said my name in the dark and it came out like a ghost 鬼 from between two trees 林. A ghost that rhymes with *a path between rice fields* which rhymes with *a piece of steamed bread* which rhymes with *paralysis of one side of the body* which rhymes with *thin blood vessels.*

In June the cicadas were so loud we thought the trees would swallow us whole.

四

It was the summer of the watermelons. They were everywhere, tumbling out of fruit shops all along the footpath. The ripest ones split open in the gutters.

Every day there is another downpour.

More than a hundred characters share the same sound.

"zong":

总 *assemble, put together / always*
踪 *footprint, trace*
鬷 *the uneven flight of a bird*

In the morning outside your apartment, the wet leaves from last night's rain had already been swept away.

五

The lady at the fruit shop asks me how I can be half Chinese and
still look like this. (She points to my hair). We come up against a
word I don't know. She draws the character in the air with one
finger and it hangs there between us.

"juan":

卷 *curl*
睠 *to have tender feeling for*
捐 *to abandon*
罥 *a net for catching birds*

六

Some things make perfect sense, like the fact that 波 (wave) is made of skin (皮) and water (氵) but most things do not.

That night there were cracks in the ceiling where the rain fell through and dripped down the back of your T-shirt, then onto my arm.

Last week two hundred white tundra swans were found dead beside a lake in Inner Mongolia.

Two days ago I smashed a glass jar of honey on the kitchen floor. The glass broke but the honey held its shards together, collapsing softly.

七

鸣 (míng), the cry of animals and insects, rhymes with tooth,
which rhymes with precipice, which rhymes with the first part of
my Chinese name.

I am full of nouns and verbs; I don't know how to live any other
way. I am a tooth-like thing. I am half sun half moon, and the
scissors used to cut away the steamed lotus leaves. I am honey
strokes spreading over the tiles.

Certain languages contain more kinds of rain than others, and I
have eaten them all.

八

The man slicing my honey pomelo has a faded tattoo of a knife on the back of his hand, the blade adjacent to his thumb.

During the seventh lunar month, when people here feed their hungry ghosts at dusk, I cut off the pieces of my hair that still smelt of smoke.

Maybe there is a word for this. I knew it once.

III.

Mother tongue / 母语

A poem in two voices

I wake to the sound of	what if my mother never left this place
blue mosque morning prayers	where the heat pours down
I have never known what the words mean	between the coconut palms
but I can hear the ache	if I had grown up here
in the kitchen every morning	I would have different-coloured hair
I peel jackfruit with my fingers	and different-coloured eyes
while they talk over and around me	I would speak to Popo all the time
in a language so familiar but so far away	we would chop vegetables together
in the kitchen every night	and peel the shells off quail eggs
I eat pink rice cakes with my hands	on blue evenings we would sit
the powdered sugar sticks to my lips	looking out for distant lightning
and Popo says *is it good?*	above the hills where plastic flowers
yes, it is good I reply in Hakka	fall against coloured graves
because it is all I can say	see how it lights up her face
and we sit there with the quiet burning	as the rain cools off the surface
of the mosquito coils	of my skin
she hands me a paper napkin	of this dream
she gestures towards her mouth	where I am not trapped
she touches my hand without speaking	in any language

Origin myths

While watching Lisa Reihana's video installation Transit of Venus [Infected]
at the Royal Academy of Art, London.

Where are you from?

What is your ethnicity?

On your mother or father's side?

How long have you been here?

How long has your family been here?

Where were you born?

Where was your mother born?

Where was your passport issued?

What is your permanent address?

What is your mother tongue?

Is your hair colour natural?

What does this country mean to you?

Is this your home?

What is the purpose of your visit today?

(In the background a woman's voice is the wind)

(Blue-green leaves shake while waves pour at my feet)

(I have never seen trees like these growing so near the sea)

(The trees and mountains are listening to the wind)

(The imaginary trees cry out)

(Singing, dancing, an endless loop of sea an endless loop of sea of sea)

(They say the sun never sets on the British Empire)

(A ship with white sails slips into the Sounds)

(A woman with feathers in her hair stands on the shore)

(Watching small volcanoes erupt slowly in the distance)

(To complete the scene I sew my own star map in red thread)

(I embroider volcanoes onto horizons)

(I stitch my name into the sea)

(I measure the distance)

Two portraits of home

After Werner's Nomenclature of Colours (1814)

[IMG_098]

morpheus butterfly wing blue   albatross white
              plastic-orchid blue   hawthorn-blossom white

                    the blue of the sounds   skimmed milk
       white
       the blue of the sounds   the blue of the sounds   unripe-mango green
                    distant-forest green   feijoa tree green
          kōwhai-petal yellow
fantail-feather cream
              volcanic grey

[IMG_227]

enamel bowl rim blue   lepidolite lilac
           throat of crocus blue

                     chrysoprase blue

magnolia-leaf green-black
plum black
           heart of jasmine pink   hot violet hot violet
purple-aster black   raspberry ice cream pink
              peach-skin pink   honey-pomelo pink
                 strawberry-wafer pink
            light blood orange
        lower wings of tiger moth red   lantern-festival red
     mooncake-wrapper gold   tūī-feather iridescent green
      electric billboard blue   neon neon green   high-definition silver
     shanghai-taxi blue   reflected-gasoline blue
                         grass-jelly black
              wet-cormorant black   nightriver black

Mixed girl's Hakka phrasebook

After Sennah Yee

Phrases I know in Hakka:

One. Two. Three. Four. Five. Sit down. It tastes good. Please. Thank you.

Phrases I don't know in Hakka:

How are you, It's so good to see you, How did you sleep, It is such a beautiful morning, Did you hear the rain, Did you have any dreams, What would you like to eat, I'm sorry, Can you speak a little slower, Can you say that again, Can you write that down, What does that mean, I can't speak, I'm sorry, I wish I could speak, How do you say, What do you know, Have you ever, Have you ever been, Have you ever seen, Have you ever felt, How long ago, When was the first time, What was it like, Do you still, Do you remember who, Do you remember the way, Do you remember when you were a child, Do you remember your home, Do you remember leaving, Do you remember the colour, Do you remember the sound of, Do you remember the taste of, Do you remember the smell of, Do you remember the name, Do you remember?

Spring onion pancakes

Hold the stalks under the tap and let the water run over your hands. Chop finely with your mum's best knife, all the way down to the white parts.

Listen to the sound the knife makes on scratched polyethylene. Let yourself go back to winter evenings spent pulling basil leaves from the dying plant by the window.

Tip in the flour, sunlight, onions, salt and rainwater. Light the flame, test the heat with the tips of your knuckles. Catch your wrist on the wok, gasp, kiss it cold.

Remember if you hadn't relearnt how to speak you would say *scallions*. Remember how she used to buy the pancakes from the market every morning, come home

and press the package into your hands, warm sesame seeds falling into your lap. Bite and feel your bones turn soft in the heat. Collect up forgotten things,

the paper towels turned transparent with grease. Gather broken eggshells into a small mountain made of calcium, then sweep the mountain away.

Some titles for my childhood memoir

After Kristen Sze-tu

the likelihood of forgetting

the dress she wore when she was young

the road to Likas Bay

the pictures that fell down in the earthquake

we could keep them

we could throw them all away

I can understand but I can't speak

no one has played that piano since

New Zealand is so far away from here

let me translate for you the poem on the wall

Styrofoam love poem

my skin gets its shine from Maggi noodle packets / golden fairy dust that glows when touching water / fluorescent lines around the edge / a girlhood seen through sheets of rainbow plastic / chemical green authentic ramen flavour / special purple packaged pho / mama's instant hokkien mee / dollar fifty flaming hearts / hands in the shape of a bowl to carry this cup of / burning liquid salt and foam / mouthful of a yellow winter morning / you shouldn't eat this shit it gives you cancer / melts your stomach lining / 99% of all this plastic comes from China / if we consume it all maybe we'll never die / never break down / I'll never be your low-carb paleo queen / I'll spike your drink with MSG / find me floating in a sea of dehydrated stars / on the surface of my steam shine dream / my plastic Chinese dream

City of forbidden shrines

I was almost born in the lunar month of padded clothing
        in the solar term of almost summer
in the season of ringing cicadas
        in the city of forbidden shrines

almost spent a girlhood watching sandstorms
        tearing through the almost golden sunlight
I almost scraped dust off my knees each day for fifteen years
        almost painted paper tigers each year to burn

I can almost hold all the meanings of 家 in my mouth
        without swallowing: [*home, family, domestic*
a *measure word* for every almost-place I've ever been]
        like the swimming pool turning almost blue
or the mausoleum of almost ten thousand oranges

here I would have never breathed an ocean
        never held mountains in my hands
                except in almost-dreams
in which long white clouds drift
        almost close enough to touch

Dialectal

This dialect has no written form / only hands feeling for a sound / only wings caught in mosquito nets / only hau sit / chau chau she says setting rice bowls on the table one in each hand / ngau heh here a handful of chopsticks dropped into the middle / I could search for characters resembling this / I could transcribe this / but there is only ahm goi / ahm sai echoing through walls / through cups reaching towards ba / towards a phone ringing / ba ma high voices melting through heat through breadfruit trees / through knuckles tapping on a marble bench saying hau sit / towards saying it back / towards letting my teeth rest on the edge of a word / not quite crossing over into / what does it taste like / say it back it it / taste of banana skin pull / taste of about to rain

What we talk about when we talk about home

lavender under the postbox   crushed seashells in the grass
          peeling ginger   in the sink
my hands feeling for   the biggest softest lemons
          waiting here   under the kōwhai

scent of báicài fried in ginger, garlic   scent of crispy chicken rice wine steam

                    breaths of   sand & salt & January sun
carried on a southern galeforce wind   to this place that always tastes the same
nothing broken nothing blown away   hello hello I can't quite hear you
hello oh it's so strange to think   it's not quite summer where you are

Black vinegar blood

For so long I didn't know how to ask for soy sauce so I dipped my dumplings in whatever was on the table, usually watered-down rice vinegar in a tiny ceramic teapot, see-through but strong enough to make my lips pucker. It dries black and sweet on my skin.

*

I order the same 饺子 every day, boiled not fried, filled with white cabbage and pork. Steam clouds curl up towards the streetlights and dissolve in the cold air along with breath and tears. He hands me vinegar in little plastic packets, two per serving. One day I'm coughing into my gloves and he gives me an extra packet, saying something I can't fully grasp but that approximates to *eat this and rest, you'll be home soon, hmm. For now have something to make your lips burn, something to warm your blood.*

*

to say the word 醋 you have to push air through your teeth
touching slightly like the start of a tsunami and pull
your lips tight in a quick kiss that never leaves the air

醋 can also mean *jealous* in the context of a love affair
and represents one of the four flavours: 酸 *(sour)*
which can also mean: *acidic, sick at heart, a tingling ache*

Happy Holiday

Tate Gallery description of Happy Holiday *by Agnes Martin*
(acrylic and graphite on canvas, 1999)

the year she left New York City and stopped painting

    she never fully uncovered

        she became translucent and light-reflecting

            she became alternating blue and pale peach

                she does not draw a distinction

                    she collapses it

                        she hovers against a field of white

                            she creates gaps in the impression

                        she is quite irregular and imperfect

                    she cannot actually exist within the natural world

Last summer we were underwater

for K.

and we asked *what are you doing there, moon?*

our bodies neck-deep in salt and rain

each crater is a sea you said & dived under

the sun before I could speak water rushing

over your skin the place where chocolate

ice cream had melted and dried there like a

newly formed freckle on the surface of

us and the islands crumbling apart softly

over sea caves somewhere opening

my mouth into the waves to say *you are*

you are you are

Conversational Chinese

[Please fill in the blanks by choosing the correct word from the list below.]

She was born in _____ in _____. She escaped to the Malaysian peninsula when she was _____ years old. Her father _____ _____. From a young age she helped her mother farm the land. She began learning a little English _____ _____. In _____ she married a handsome marine biology student. She had three children, two daughters and one son, all of whom attended the local Christian Chinese school. In the evenings she sat under the _____ tree in her backyard, rinsing and peeling _____ into a _____ bowl, watching her youngest son chase her eldest daughter around the grass with a cicada tied to the end of a piece of string. Some years later, when the _____ started up in the streets, she looked at the sea and longed to send her children across it, far away, where they would be _____, where she would one day visit them.

Shenzhen / Guangzhou / Xiamen / 1928 / 1929 / 1931
five / six / nine / eight / died shortly after / did not join them
fell ill on board / in high school / from a stranger / by teaching herself
1953 / 1954 / 1956 / mango / breadfruit / yellow flame coconut
ginger / turmeric root / daikon / wintermelon
turquoise / aquamarine / seafoam / sirens / shouting
loudspeakers / fires / in her prayers / happy / safe

[Please answer the following questions in full sentences.]

你的外婆在哪里出生？

Mum says it isn't really clear where she was born, but most likely somewhere near Shenzhen.

你的外婆什么时候来到马来西亚？

We think she came by boat along with her mother and father, but we think her father may have died on the journey, or somehow didn't make it.

你的外婆在哪里入土为安？

They scattered her ashes over the sea off the coast of Kota Kinabalu, within sight of the blue mountain made of clouds.

Dreaming in a language I can't speak

This is not a souvenir.
This is not what it looks like.

Her name 《 雯 》
means *multi-coloured clouds.*

I almost tattooed it on my skin
while explaining over and over

this is what you can't see:
pieces of language that fell out of my mouth

as a child, crushed-up words I pull back
from disappearing rooms inside disappearing homes,

the name my grandfather gave me 《 明雅 》
two characters I still cannot write beautifully—

    a sun 日 next to a moon 月
    a tooth 牙 next to a bird 隹

She gave me a seal with my name carved inside it.
In a room full of untouched sunlight

I let hot wax drip onto my palm
leaving a mark that will fade over time

like the imprint of rain
in burnt chrysanthemum clouds.

In the dream-mirror
I open my mouth

and birds fly out from between my teeth.
They do not make a sound.

April Kōwhai

When the April heatwave came, my mum sent a WeChat video from Malaysia of an evening downpour. You can't see the rain, only the effects of it: a gasp from her mouth and a yellow flame tree reflected in the wet, shaking.

/

I see a yellow blur from far away and walk closer, disbelieving. Here is a kōwhai tree on the edge of a garden in North London, in full bloom. For a moment I do not breathe air, I breathe yellow, I breathe myself home.

/

My phone is vibrating, telling me: *You have a new memory.* Here is a stream of pictures collected into an album, all taken somewhere far away. Home is not a place but a string of colours threaded together and knotted at one end.

/

Kōanga, *springtime*, often synonymous with kōwhai, *yellow*. In another time and place, I watch the hills above the house turn gold.

/

When people say things like *the hottest April day in sixty years* it becomes necessary to make note of the bright heat of the concrete, the fallen magnolias with their shy blood roots, the fingernail kōwhai blooms curling translucently like discarded chrysalids. Be still. You have a new memory.

/

Ua kōwhai, light spring showers, or: kōwhai showers—when the world becomes a sea of yellow. I now know it can happen anywhere, even somewhere cold.

/

In her childhood bedroom my mum slides back the mosquito net and holds her phone against windowpane, recording the rain.

Sonnet with particles of gold

Today scientists discovered the origins of gold:
the sound of egg noodles crisping up in the wok,
the garden carpeted in kōwhai petals,
the way my phone corrects raumati (*summer*) to *rainstorm*.
The day after my grandmother died was white-gold in colour.
A star explodes and wings are found among the debris
along with pieces of a character I never memorised—
our only name for her, 婆, a woman 女 beneath a wave 波.
"Drift," she mouths softly in English, "what is *drift*?"
My mother translates into her language, not one of mine.
I try to make myself remember by writing 婆 over and over
on squares of paper covering the walls so I am surrounded
by the women and the water radicals they hold close.
The tips of waves touch me in my sleep.

Alternate words for mixed-race

After Danez Smith

Mudblood.[1]
Hapa.[2]
"Nǐ shìbushì hùnxuè?" [3]
A string of plastic chrysanthemums.[4]
My body's made of crushed little stars.[5]
A bowl of tangerines left on the blue grave at dusk.[6]
"Can I guess your ethnicity?" [7]
An apparition; a faint trace of something; a faint secondary image
produced by a fault in an optical system.[8]
"A stroke is missing here. Can't you write your own name?" [9]
When I think of that word [half-caste], I get an image in my head of being split
and split again to the point where you just shimmer like glitter.[10]
明雅 is not my middle name but my second first name. My name.[11]
I try again but I am left holding a bird in one hand
and a halved moon in the other.[12]

---

[1] When you described yourself with this word one night over Hainan
chicken rice in the fluorescent shopping mall, I started to laugh—

[2] Not included in the document "Terms Used to Describe People of
'Mixed-Race': Past and Present" compiled by the *Multiple Heritage
Project* in 2009.

[3] In a stationary shop down a hutong in Beijing, shaking snow out of my
hair, the shop attendant approaches me with her fingers outstretched.

[4] These mourning flowers are always either yellow or white.

[5] Mitski Miyawaki, from her album *Puberty 2*.

[6] We bought mini tangerines at the market and unpeeled and ate them
two at a time.

[7] Standing in the crowd in the rooftop bar, the stars are about to burst
over my head.

[8] I don't believe in ghosts but I believe people who say they have seen them.

[9] *Please present a report on your exchange in Beijing with a title page and
photographs attached.*

[10] Tayi Tibble, in an interview with digital-serum.com.

[11] *Bright / elegance.* I split the pieces into smaller pieces: a sun next to a
moon / a tooth next to a bird.

[12] A close variant of 雅 is 鴉, crow.

The first wave

14 November 2016

they request that we inform you immediately   you are standing on soft ground
                    the ceiling lights are swinging in the background
        the waves crash, then dissipate   the first wave may not be the largest
this is a flow-on event so do not go near   do not stay and watch the land
        slipping   it has triggered other faults like a network of nerves
and the seabed has risen out of the sea   there are visible ruptures
running along the landscape   this is a flow-on event
but the moon does not cause earthquakes   the ceiling lights are a typical pattern
        of aftershocks   and they request that we inform you
                    you are a visible rupture running along the landscape
do not stay and watch   your nerves slipping
        there will be strong currents in the background
the moon has risen out of the sea   the first wave crashes, then dissipates
                    you are standing on such soft ground

Magnolia, jade orchid, she-wolf

Magnolia: the most ancient flowering tree known to mankind, of the plant family *Magnoliaceae,* has survived ice ages, continental drifts, mountain formations.

/

Each day we watch the petals fall. Thick white pieces of skin on the pavement all over Shanghai, their scent crushed into the air.

/

Her name means *magnolia,* yet in the Disney movie, cherry blossoms fill the screen.

/

Back home in spring, they are everywhere, flaming in the corners of my vision. Leafless, blushing, open-mouthed by the sea. Doused in pink, tongues out.

/

Mùlán: 木兰 (simplified) or 木蘭 (traditional). Composed of 木 which means *wood,* and 蘭 which means *orchid.* Not to be confused with the similarly pronounced múláng 母狼, *she-wolf.*

/

The official flower of the city of Shanghai: dark trees with ghost-white buds haunt courtyards and avenues. At night they loom and glow.

/

I try to study the trees so I can name them, so I can remember them. Magnolia, ginkgo, plane. Magnolia, ginkgo, plane.

/

I want to know the names of the trees in all other languages to so that I find out what they taste like to other people. But my mouth can only hold so much.

/

The first movie I watched with a Chinese character in it was *Mulan*. To help me practice, we watched it in Chinese but I understood none of the words.

/

It was a glorious Saturday afternoon when I set foot in the garden. A faint cool breeze was sweeping in from the river, blowing away the mist and clouds. Magnolia blossoms were in full bloom, dotting the tree like giant white-ribbon bows fringed by dark-green leaves.

Adeline Yen Mah, *Chinese Cinderella*

/

In Year 7 we read *Chinese Cinderella*. Before her name was Adeline, it was Jun-ling. We are not given the Chinese characters of her name. My teacher asked me to help her pronounce the foreign words.

/

Mùlán, yínxìng, xuánlíngmù.

/

Magnolia denudata, lilytree or *yulan magnolia.* Native of central and eastern China. Petals curved like swans' necks, with faint lines of blood around the roots. This species is called yùlán, *jade orchid.*

/

In the country where I was born, the trees are a different language. A language I am trying to learn. Karaka, mānuka, kōwhai. Karaka, mānuka, kōwhai.

/

Mum gave me a heart of jade wrapped in pink and yellow threaded silk. It belonged to her step-grandmother, whose name I don't know, who walked under the magnolia trees of Shanghai.

/

In Aotearoa, jade is called pounamu or greenstone. The stones are sacred taonga, found in rivers.

/

glorious

        river

    in full bloom,

                    fringed by

  dark-green

/

Mùlán, yínxìng, xuánlíngmù. My mouth a river in full bloom.

Notes

The title of this poetry collection is written in traditional Chinese characters. In simplified Chinese, 木蘭 is written as 木兰, pronounced 'mùlán' in Mandarin.

'Letter from Shanghai', 1938 quotes lines from New Zealand poet Robin Hyde's travel memoir *Dragon Rampant* (AG Books, 2013), about her experiences reporting on the Sino-Japanese War in China.

'*The Great Wall* (2016)' refers to the movie of the same name directed by Zhang Yimou and starring Matt Damon.

'Falling City' is about the life and work of the writer Eileen Chang (1920-1995) who was born in Shanghai, in a part of the city then known as the Shanghai International Settlement. She began publishing short stories, novellas and essays in magazines in her early twenties and rose to fame during the Japanese occupation of Shanghai, which began in 1937 and ended with the surrender of Japan in August 1945. This poem quotes from the following sources: 'The Golden Cangue' and 'Love in a Fallen City' both from *Love in a Fallen City* translated by Karen S. Kingsbury (New York Review of Books, 2006).

'Dark violets' quotes lines from a sign located at Yunnan Ethnic Village theme park (云南民族村) in Kunming, China.

'Rain episodes' quotes from the afterword of *The Woman Warrior: Memoirs of a Girlhood Among Ghosts* by Maxine Hong Kingston (Picador, 2015).

'Last eclipse' is a found poem partly composed of lines from the essay 'Total Eclipse' by Annie Dillard, from her collected essays *The Abundance* (Canongate, 2017).

'Magnolia, jade-orchid, she-wolf' quotes lines from *Chinese Cinderella* by Adeline Yen Mah (Puffin Books, 1999).

Acknowledgements

Thank you to the editors of the following publications where earlier versions of these poems first appeared: *POETRY, Hotel, Mimicry, The Margins, Pain, The Pantograph Punch, Starling, The Rialto, Rambutan Literary, Daikon, Hainamana Arts, close, The Shanghai Literary Review, Shabby Doll House, Scum, wildness* and *New Zealand Poetry Shelf.*

'Field notes on a downpour' was published as a limited-edition pamphlet by If A Leaf Falls Press in 2018.

I am grateful for the friendship and generosity of writers Helen Rickerby, Jennifer Wong, Pema Monaghan, Jay G. Ying, Jessica J. Lee, Rose Lu and Alison Wong, many of whom were first readers of these poems. This book is also for the Shanghai poets: David, Aiden, Patrick, Lei and Janel.

I completed this book with support from the Rebecca Swift Foundation and the Women Poets' Prize 2018. I'm also indebted to Education New Zealand and Victoria University of Wellington for two scholarships that enabled me to live and study in Shanghai, where most of these poems were written.